Dreamscape Journeys

Poems

Jakob Brønnum

Cyberwit.net
HIG 45 Kaushambi Kunj, Kalindipuram
Allahabad - 211011 (U.P.) India
http://www.cyberwit.net
Tel: +(91) 9415091004
E-mail: info@cyberwit.net

Printed at Repro India Limited.

I stare into the sun

But never in the mirror

(Taylor Swift)

Foreword

This is a poetry collection consisting of dreams and surrealist paintings. I have been trying to arrange these meetings between the poems and the dream for quite a while. Early on in the process, I realized that the surrealist painters, from whom I received much inspiration on the way to this collection, did provide a kind of bridge. In the collection there are poems on Dalí, de Chirico, and Magritte.

It literally took two years for me to realize that the collection needed balancing from two longer suites of poems on subjects, directing to the dream, and to the state of being awake, but encapsulated by the symbolism of the dream, although dissolving.

The book opens with the suite entitled Études Mélodiques (Melodic Studies) and closes with the suite Parallel Souls. They are directly indebted to two works of music, paraphrasing these works in poetry. The works are Marie Awadis' Études melodiques (Deutsche Gramophone 2024) and Laura Pausini: Anime Parallele (Parallel Souls) (Warner Music 2023), with the titles in Pausini translated into English. The titles in the poems are taken from the titles in the musical compositions.

The book is illustrated with three works of de Chirico that have been a great inspiration for a long time. Dreamscape Journeys is a companion volume to my book The Poetry Encyclopedia of Dreams (Cyberwit 2025).

JB, January 2025

Contents

Études Mélodiques 9
About Dalí 21
Dreams, Uncaught 22
The Burden 24
Dreaming Again About Going Around in Our House 25
Naked Bodies 26
The Hen and the Dog 27
The Lizard and the Ladybug 28
The Glass Bell in the Tree 29
The Birds in the Gutter 31
Fields of Eggs 32
What I Didn't Say 33
War and Me and my Mother 34
The Cylinder over the House 35
Wardreaming 36
Halfway Out on the Bridge 37
The Keys and the Echoes 38
Pink, They Said 39
Face in Blue 40
Broken Mirror Glass 41
The Dream Where I Showed the King and Queen 42
And Poetry 43
Some People Do Not Hear Birds in the Morning 45
Poor Next-Level Soul 46
Trying to Get Home by Train 47
The Stairs 48
Lost in the City 49
I Want to Dream in de Chirico's Landscapes 52
Walking the Hallway 53
The View from the Backseat 54
The Orange Triangles 55

The Big Dog in the Public Square 56
Hands in Dreams 57
The Funeral Procession 58
Scapegoat 59
My Parents 61
The Hotel 62
Magrittescape 63
The Dream about Lazarus, Martha, and Mary 64
Parallel Souls (Dream Meetings) 65
Acknowledgements 85
Books by Jakob Brønnum 86

Études Mélodiques
(The Grand Dream Scenario)

Étude No. 1: Playing Games

The grand dream scenario has begun
like the opening sequence
you are in fact the protagonist (and the villain)

you thought you couldn't sleep
but now you are in the middle of the dream of your life
the dream you shall not forget

because it wants to get a grip on you
and you will let it, you will let it
because you are one for playing games

and no-one will be able to
blow your cover
because it's all in a dream

Étude No. 2: Breathless

In the dream I could not breathe
after a while I thought
I had died, I was falling, falling

In the dream I was breathless
from joy, and then again breathless from fear
and then I woke up

I woke up in the dream
but I was still dreaming. I laughed
at my dream as if it were another person

Étude No. 3: Ballade

When we were young, oh yes,
all the phantoms that surrounded us
wherever we looked

They owned castles in my nightmares
empty rooms, doors opening
behind me, shrieking, and long shadows falling

until I discovered everything
was a ghost of my imagination, witchcraft
from beyond my consciousness

I was doomed to stride
the barren landscapes searching
for places where the music might be

Étude No. 4: Empty Rooms

In Room no. 1 I saw traces of dust
in the floor as if there were people
hanging around, discussing
secrets of mine, secrets of theirs

In Room no. 2 there were no windows

in No. 3 cobwebs covered the ceiling
I was given the key to No. 5
but I never found it

I kept stopping at No. 4
where I knew the beautiful one
was living with her aunt
or another close relative, her grandmother

probably. When I opened the door
the room was empty, of course

Room no. 6 had mirrors for walls
Room no. 7 was mine. It had no doors

Étude No. 5: Traces

There were traces of voices
in the corridor
traces of dust on my imagination
traces of thoughts
in the next dream scenario
there was debris, fallen trees
lost feathers from doves
wobbling down through the silence
of the woods. The air was pure

And you heard your ravens

We feared one of them might be gone
but now they were both there

Étude No. 6: La Forêt Oubliée

I saw a young woman in the turquoise spectrum
nearer green than blue
pouring water
from a glass bowl

onto the ground. With every drop
a tree sprang from somebody's imagination

All trees have a secret life,
all life has a secret tree

In the turquoise spectrum
there is a forgotten forest floating

in the turquoise spectrum
between the sky and the underground

Étude No. 7: Exodus

I tried to make a list of what
to throw out

but I discovered
I was making a list of what was lost

in the meantime
the dream was loading

I never got to keep
any of the images for myself

I had to put them
in a box of my own

I chose my memory
unfortunately

since it is not reliable
but it's the only thing I've got

Étude No. 8: Through the Window

There was a song about the raven
outside the window right at midnight

at that time most of what is outside
seems to be much closer than it really is

In the long summer nights
sometimes we hear the trains

knowing that they will make their syncopated
journey on the steel lines of our hearts

for as long as we dream

Étude No. 9: Unspoken Words

In dreams you always discover
the words that were meant to be said

as they draw their lines on the wall of glass
you cannot go through. Sometimes

you wish the dream would allow you
to do things you cannot do awake

and when it does on rare occasions
it never is quite what you had in mind

You stand before the wall of glass waiting
they way life taught you about waiting

the same way it taught you about
being hungry, and tired, and acting kind

Étude No. 10: Void

The important dream is about turning around the void
from the darkness everything falls into

as soon as the scenery changes
to the unknown sequences of light

and music from bells of brass and water
are dripping onto the very old trunks of future

This is the void: There is no void. There is time
This is time: There is no space. There is being

Étude No. 11: l'Horloge des Rêves

The dream ticking through past nights
trying to trigger you

you never know what you remember tomorrow

but you know that somewhere
in your memory it all lies preserved

Death will carry it further along. In due course
some of it will go to waste

Étude No. 12: Unveiled

Until then you shall wander
like Cain in the outskirts of your mind whenever
you seek rest
on white pillows of silence

Time, and the motor of dreams
which we cannot control
will decide what you will meet
along the way

The dream is no priest
but then time is no coincidence

About Dalí

Dreams are bred in secrecy. Dalí showed me
how dreams do exist outside those enclosures of mysticism

A body in a desert, distant scenic light transcendent
his neck drawn out, supported by a crutch

like a joke about unspoken pain
and unspeakable longing

Dalí likes to tell jokes
not all of them particularly good

if you complain about the joke
he'll claim it was self-deprecatory

Then he puts an elephant in there as well
a white elephant with no particular persona

This is where my dreams originated
like fragments not destined to be collected

in a whiteness beyond the possibility of death

Dreams, Uncaught

What, then, is a dream? I perceive objects,
yet there is nothing. I see men. I think that I speak
to them and hear them answer me,
yet there is no one and I say nothing.

Henri Bergson, The World of Dreams

So many dreams I don't catch
and suddenly
they show themselves
like when I'm in the garden
picking up apples
from the ground
and hear apples falling
behind me
as I bend down
to reach into the grass
the long, long grass of blue September

The Burden

Often in the afternoon
I lie on the couch

reading, or drinking coffee
in the unrepairable
sense of having taken

somebody's life
in a dream a while ago

even though I didn't,
I know exactly how it feels

yet again and again I'm reminded
by my faithful subconsciousness

about the hole I made
in everything

Dreaming Again About Going Around in Our House

So many rooms we never used
I will count them when I dream the dream again

scrutinizing the bookshelves I never knew we had
searching the storeroom under the staircase
where you found the stash of candlesticks
from your grandmother in her exile

Wait, I shall try to locate the string of pearls
that hung from the ceiling one time
telling me about my mother's childhood in Berlin in the 1920s

You have those dreams, too. I never met you in my dream. Why?
Throughout all the dream I know you are in the house

Maybe one day we will dream
the same dream about going around in our house
never to meet and when we want
to tell the other about it in the morning
we'd let the other begin, and in the meantime
listening to the other's dream, we forgot our own

I wonder what it's like outside our house in my dream
I wonder why the curtains are always drawn

Naked Bodies

I rarely dream about naked bodies. I remember
one time, 13 years old or slightly younger
I dreamt about the more graceful older sister of someone I knew

it must have touched something embryonic in me
I had not consciously met awake

Swimming naked in the sea high above me, her female body

the turquoise water and her fine skin
the urge to reach her, knowing I had no means
obviously still lacking the notion
of the holy symbiosis
between passion and possession

I clearly remember the gracious movement of her nameless body
I clearly remember the dream executing the electrifying feeling

I carry with me to this day

The Hen and the Dog

I dream about the hen and the dog
spinning, dancing, twirling

around each other
Noise and plumage fill the air.

Taking a break, the two of them stare at each other
making hilarious postures on the gravel road

But are they even speaking the same body language?
Sometimes the hen makes this curious jump straight up in the air

everybody laughs (except the hen
devoid of wings as she is, but not of anxiety)

sometimes the dog tries to break its leash to get to her
breathlessly straining his neck till the bark is just a squeak.

Sometimes they love each other, showing real patience
and affection. But it takes so long to come around to that

that by then I'm usually on my way home
kicking gravel on the pathway as I walk

The Lizard and the Ladybug

The lizard still watches the ladybug
the question about the meal unanswered

The Glass Bell in the Tree

I passed the tree with the glass bell
I seem to remember it from somewhere

though I have never seen it before
typical of my dreams to make these plays with memory

The sound of the glass bell:
a whole and undisturbed tone

spreading its wings over the garden
I did not hear it when I first passed

only when I hesitated before passing by again
Why did I suddenly hesitate?

I said to myself: There are no birds
in the garden this morning

There is no morning, it dawned on me. Not today
only the glass bell in the tree
The Writing on the Wall

Why do I arrive too late
to read the writing on the wall. Why am I always late

in my dream, never in time
for reading the writing on the wall

letters seeping away
as I approach

the wall. I say to myself: You never run fast enough
in your dream, do you?

You just watch as your thought
dissolves before you

and then bang your head
on the wall

The Birds in the Gutter

I was looking for birds in the gutter
I was looking for birds
in the street
I was looking for birds way above the chimneys

It was like when you try to catch
a sheet of paper
in the wind
and the wind shows you what willpower really is

There were no birds
in the gutter
and no birds in the street
only fallen leaves. I had no use for them

I was looking for birds. Still looking

Fields of Eggs

Who are the others walking these fields of eggs
I only see their skin-colored silhouettes
their shadowy bones

everybody has been here one time or other
all might not remember
their fields of eggs

The dream shall call upon the memory
in due time, the worm, the snake

the alien, the Sunday mornings, the voice of mother
long gone, still heard in the other room

What I Didn't Say

I didn't say I didn't want to

I didn't say I saw you
I didn't say you went away
I didn't
I didn't say I didn't

I saw you
then
but it's not now

it is like time in dreams
it is not there

War and Me and my Mother

I more often dream about war
than about my mother

though sometimes she makes
a form of appearance

her shadow always
just left the room

And so it is: Outside a war is raging
everything is in ruins

but not the way it is in here

The Cylinder over the House

We were sleeping outside on the porch
there was no difference between house and garden

(sometimes there isn't)

I woke when the large cylinder
passed right above the trees

and as I made for the inside
to take refuge

another vessel loaded with micro electronics
landed in front of the house

men pouring out
directing sensory instruments

towards our home and us
you sensed no danger

I tried in vain to find a way to suggest to you
that we hurried back to sleep

Wardreaming

I seem to never dream about how they will get food to the soldiers behind enemy lines or how they carry the young boys home. I dream about the bombers that are coming soon, and I even see them on the horizon. Forces so strong I know the only thing to do is try to hide. Flee and hide. Hide and flee while everything falls into its war-torn state and the dream is all about how to get back

Halfway Out on the Bridge

Not knowing if it will bear
halfway out on the bridge

there is no rain to dissolve the fog
there is no way to see my steps

there is no time of day
no tunnel of night, no hall of night

you have to rely on yourself
in these kinds of situations

talk with the body that you hate
Why do I hate my body in my dream?

And why this strange dream?
Is this a bridge to friendship?

Is there going to be hope on the other side
or do I have to cling to it here

Not knowing if it will bear
halfway out on the bridge

The Keys and the Echoes

My keys were sitting out there
in the front door all night

inside, shoes were soaked
the fridge laid off. Water running

down the floor. No mice
this time. All the doors were open

down the hallway
echoes I didn't notice

before I woke up, realizing
everything was normal, and nothing

missing, out of the ordinary

Pink, They Said

When sufficiently tired you know how to walk around
between the middle albums of Pink Floyd
floating in collections of ancient poems
paning between unknown works of abstract expressionism
staring wide-eyed on mornings with megalomanic windows

torn apart by rain drops
as elegant as suppressed tears

memories, standing like statues of Easter Island
aligned with a coast of empty imagination

some have tumbled, some have flown away
some blew up in an earlier dream

Face in Blue

In dreams I see a face in blue
not being able to tell the difference
between the color, the face
or the shadow of the soul it depicts

When I wake up, this question:

does eternity manifest itself in dreams
or is the face just a mark of time

And this:
Do shadows have a place in space
or do they just blur certain spans of time

Broken Mirror Glass

But why am I trying to mend the broken mirror
making it into a cup I could drink from? But why

am I trying to mend the broken mirror glass
making it a pool of water, thinking:

Just a little pool of water,
somebody might find peace and quiet there

Why am I picking up broken glass from beneath
that old mirror in the hallway

it hung in my mother's childhood home?
Why am I getting no cuts on my fingers?

And why am I so shameful about the broken mirror.
I didn't break it, the dream broke it

The Dream Where I Showed
the King and Queen

The dream where I showed the king and queen my little bike
In spite of the small wheels, it goes very fast. They must think
I'm very good at biking. I asked them about it. They agreed.

They are very kind people.

Unfortunately, some dirt from the gravel road sprayed unto
their lawn while I took one of my turns. They didn't like that.

I wonder what they do now
and if they still remember me

And Poetry

No emails about poetry
no emails written
just like poems

no poems ever arrive by email

none of the emails
I receive
even in my dreams
are poems,

with little empty spaces inside the meaning of the whole
for you or me to fill out

little black spots inside each word
to be found only by incident

Some People Do Not Hear Birds in the Morning

They wake up and there is nothing
there might be a distant motor or a door slamming

but silence is not truly broken
there are no birds

some people sit up in bed, rubbing their eyes, curtains drawn
knowing their dream has been mocking them with birds

they are able to look briefly back in time, down into it
like being able to see whatever's behind you

or like walking, holding hands
with time as if you were lovers

Poor Next-Level Soul

There is dark matter, a cluster of no-go
a realm of deep and grey nothingness

stealing my identity
and I trust it must be a dream

and that I will wake up again some morning
other than this. But there is no other

because there is no morning
in the first place

Trying to Get Home by Train

I am always trying to get home by train
sometimes I discover I forgot my luggage in the hotel

or I realize I'm not going to make my connection
and have no way to reach you since my phone is dead

If you only knew how often I have sprung from car to car
on the train without finding somebody in a uniform.

Often, I leave the train station to try and find a connection
by bus, but the bus never comes

Often, I find myself endlessly stalking
the train station but they keep changing the track

In all these dreams I have never ever been contacted
by anybody or talked to someone myself

The Stairs

Well, I suppose we cannot let it off anymore
we have to talk about the stairs
I never see them
like they looked before the bulb broke
it will be like this forever
nobody will ever come to change it
it cannot happen
it is not cosmologically mapped out

It is as if I never get to walk the stairs in my dream
as if I know that I shall walk
the stairs
when the dream is over

and I'm not there any longer
Can't we just talk about the knees? No

Lost in the City

1

I dream about a city I don't know
little by little I realize it is the place I recently moved to

I know I don't have the address
I didn't memorize it yet

I have no means of finding home. There are no
telephones. Just people and supermarkets, subway stations

just people going past me. Then I wake up.
Then I dream the dream again

2

I often wonder why it is in the city
I am lost, never the desert

with no walls or shelter
where all lines in the landscape

mime the others. It seems
never to be a labyrinth

under the old house
or in my school with all the stairs

where we went up and down
year in and year out

3

If there ever was somewhere I was really lost
it was in school

I never dream about it. I did at one point
but it stopped. I don't dream about

my mother anymore either. I just dream
about being lost in the city

where I have decided to live

I Want to Dream in de Chirico's Landscapes

I want to dream in de Chirico's landscapes
maybe they are not landscapes but mind-scapes

I want to dream there, so I can walk around
and choose my towers, my statues

my columns, my green horizon, my locomotives
my gloves, my stool, my trains

In de Chirico's landscapes there are no voices
only the thoughts you catch while you walk them

Walking the Hallway

It seemed to continue forever, this hallway. Doors lined the hallway. Every door was open when I saw it but closed as I passed. Light flooding from beyond, heavy noise or this stillness as quiet as only death. But where is beyond in a dream? And how can you differ between noise and quiet in a dream? Do you understand you're dreaming just because the dream tells you so? The only thing the dream did not question was me walking. Walking the hallway. It was like that. I had to walk the hallway, like maybe forever, doors lining the hallway, open when I see them, closed as I pass

The View from the Backseat

For years I was driving around
in the backseat of somebody's car
several times a week in my dreams

sometimes with the sense that I should
have taken more responsibility
for this venture

knowing that was precisely
what I could not accomplish
at that time. I was in the backseat

There is never a full view
from the backseat, but I sensed
we were going was seriously downhill

The Orange Triangles

I finally found it, the place
where the orange triangles appeared

I looked for children with balloons
dancing in the open space between the warehouses

men walking, neon-clad
the trumpets in the background

everybody anxiously
awaiting horses, though only bulldozers arrive

I saw no children. No trumpets sounded
Some of the orange triangles

modulated into balloons

The Big Dog in the Public Square

There is a dog. It is big. He (must be a he?)
is sitting in the public square

lots of people talking and laughing about something
I can't hear. I know it's a he. It's in his gaze

I can't move. I need to wait and see if he is a dog that bites
The dream doesn't seem to mind these watchful

moments. But I do. Could I maybe trust the dream to help? Please!
I wonder what they are talking about in the beautiful square

what fine voices they have, these girls in the sun
Timelessness. Timelessness, Timelessness. Still these unfathomable

voices in the square, in the sun. The beautiful sun. Dog staring at me
You really can't trust a dream to warn you about a dog and its
temper, can you?

You really can't expect a dream to let you hear all the ringing
voices in the square. Especially not with the dog around

Hands in Dreams

Like the way hands are never
present as mirrors of my thoughts

when they are really needed
like in this dream full of doubt

you never have full control over them
in dreams. As if you go around in there

unbalanced, untimely, unchecked

The Funeral Procession

People stopped their cars
and went out to let it pass in silence

there was a casket clad in foliage
the rain was singing

people's emotions painting all the houses grey
the deceased wasn't present

In the end the sun came out
to tell everybody about the end of the day

Scapegoat

Certain dreams you realize you were waiting for. For
how long? There was a goat
falling off the cliff

Who did it? These questions the dream never answers

it puts them to you
and then leave you in the desert

wandering around looking for the carcass

My Parents

I really am trying to remember
my parents in dreams

I hear my father's voice
listening to Haydn in his mornings

the voice creeps slightly above the violins
in the string quartet

as a fifth instrument, or sixth
if you count the morning

Sometimes I discover my mother
behind a tree or in the next room

waiting for me to come in? Or to pass?
These are things I shall not know

I really am trying to remember
my parents in dreams

So many things I shall not know

The Hotel

& I can't find my room
because I'm on the wrong floor
& I forgot the room number
because my key is out of sight
& I don't know where the elevator stops

I must calculate the floor
since the elevator has no panel telling me about it

I used not to be alone in here
but now I am

& you are waiting in the room
I know you are

Magrittescape

Nobody wants to dream a painting by Magritte
even though you might somehow
imagine it'd be a cool thing to go through

Warning: Don't lend any hope to Magritte, nor dreams

Why? If there was ever one not to lend your dreams to
it was he. He will crush any dream

make it consist of bits of itself all alike, they just don't fit
together. He will make the dream constantly stop
and then begin all over again. That will be perpetual. He will pretend
to laugh because he knows you are human. But he is only

pretending. And all you hear
is the ha-ha-ha. He will not be there.

He will have left by then. It is forbidden, to laugh in a Magrittescape
he knows because he makes the rules. And now
you know it, too. Even if you thought
you might want to draw up a couple of rules
for yourself, be advised: There is no room
for additional rules where Magritte has been canvassing

The Dream about Lazarus, Martha, and Mary

The Dutch tradition of showing
the meeting from the kitchen
everything is being transformed from
the word to excessive eating

Tintoretto paints the scene
with Mary sitting by the feet of the Lord preaching
Martha comes to ask her to help
peel the potatoes

I fear being trapped inside the opposite of reality
Sometimes I dream I am Martha,
other times I am clearly Mary.
On rarer occasions it boils down to Lazarus

with the cloth around my face

Parallel Souls (Dream Meetings)

1.
Ciao

Nobody ever truly shows themselves
in a greeting on a sloping street

Nobody ever truly shows themselves
not on purpose. We do

live here, parallel souls
whose ways might never cross

2
You will take yourself far

I see you on a street
of fantasy, sweet dreams
and science fiction

The way you are so much
greater than I am (greater than me?)

The way you are so much better
at smiling, at holding your head

the right way
at the right time

so much better at parrying
warding off currents

You live beneath
skyscrapers

3
A good start

A good start does in no way
guarantee an acceptable finish

My dream will go AWOL
and I am in it

You're in it too

4
Last

Anytime light imposes
itself on your eyes
you know it will last a lifetime

Anytime somebody
imposes emotions upon you
you know it will last till it's over again

Between light and emotions
only the images from your parallel dreams
and your intertwined lives will last

5

The first step on the moon

Not rarely
I have this dream about
everybody being
the first person on the moon

I don't mean to say
all were there at the same time

but little by little,
little by little, little
by little

6
Zero

Much of what we do comes down to this
and it shows in our dreams

Still, it is not meaningless

In our dreamscape journeys
we lived parallel lives
but outside of that
outside of those illusions
these days were all we had

all there was

7
Natural home

Where we live together, becoming
part of each other's symbols
of life. There are trees above us

but never without leaves falling
like snow and rain

like shared memories

8
Enemy

Is the moon the enemy
of the sun? Is night
the enemy of day?

You are not my enemy
my sweet companion
my parallel soul

I am my enemy
putting shadows in front of you
and in front of myself

9.
To our love [to]

Because of the begotten
because of the imagined sky
in the vein of the vibrant blood
you never carry
through your night bridges
in the aura of archaic symbolism
because of the sisterhood of the moon

and of the morning
and of the birds hiding from us
yet assuring us they
are here

10
Every time

Every time I see you
my dreams blend with my notion
of being alive
not alone, every time
another instance
of shared daylight

tell me about the whys
and the maybes

and how I ask them
every time
in order to melt into all the time

11
Parallel souls

There are dreams and there
are dreams
& there are souls and
there are souls
& there are streets and there are streets

there are streets:
parallel streets where we walk
while we look at each other

walking on the other side
of the street

& of the soul
& in the mirror

12
Yet it is not like that

Singularly imagining the fall
we are sure it will come
and often also when

The second fall
the third fall

But with our souls aligned
this knowledge
vaporizes
in the voids between

our minds

13
What is it

Again, we ask these questions
that cannot be answered
but we demand they wait for us
regardless of consequence

Again, we ask. And when we try
to answer before the echo has rung out
we get these half-baked truths

Again, we ask. And when
we aim at finding the answers
and keeping them secret

we find we have been left behind.
It is not there anymore
We shall never know what it is

14
More than an idea

We were more than an idea
we were leaves falling from the trees

We are more than an idea
we will be hands seeking hands

We will remain more than an idea
we believe that breath
as breath, drawn breath

cannot truly go away

15
But

Hope is the only ingredient necessary
for this to materialize

the sense of belonging
comes with the breeze

radiance aligned in hope
suspended in what we cannot see

16
Flashback

These dreams have the ability to do for us
what we always want
but never dare hope for or establish
as a fact: That everything exists simultaneously

that no linguistic tense
may send any impressions, emotions, and actions
out of our reality
of being here, right now

The pressure is different, the journey will vary

the spirit will be dormant
every so often

17
Venus

Every dream has this light
falling out of the sky, falling nowhere
Venus, the light with no obvious purpose
though it has function

She was the one who was always missed
when we walked across the field
down the pathway
together. How often did we forget to breathe

and let the body remember
because we trusted

Was that Venus lurking? The she-ness, the she-scape,
flowing through the dream like invisible water

18
It's worth it

Because we never forgot that we lived the same life
because days were spent
never totally devoid of animals
in the vicinity of mind
by the sound of water, close by or in active remembrance

because on a few occasions we managed
things together
that made all the sorrow
seem to have had a purpose

absolution of sorrow is a theme
that cannot be defined and only emotionally acknowledged

19
Beyond the surface

Like water, like drowning, like
flowing in a lake
beyond everyday matters

like when your face is not observed
the same way anymore

That almost forgotten moment
when the dreamscape journey
promised you a freedom it did not point to

so you had to find it yourself
after the fact, beyond the surface

20
Before us

Before us is everything, and nothing

every symbol of birth and transition
every breath we shared during last autumn

everything we saw together
without noticing time

every trace of music in the leaves
every dead bird on the porch

before us dreams of uprightness so hard to recall
dreams of broken rhythm
dreams of surviving, before us everything

and nothing

Acknowledgements

About Dalí, Walking the Hallway and Scapegoat have been published in the magazine Masticadores October-November 2024

The Glass Bell in the Tree, The Writing on the Wall, The Birds in the Gutter have been published in the Taj Mahal Review December 2024

Sincere thanks are due to Kathrina Martinsen for her work with the manuscript

Books by Jakob Brønnum

A little book of transcendence (2023)

The Road to Tremonte (2024)

The Poetry Encyclopedia of Dreams (2025)

Dreamscape Journeys (2025)